A M A Z I N G
SPACE
FACTS

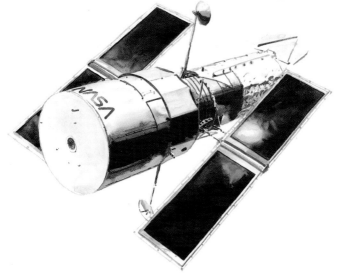

Nicholas Booth and Heather Amery
Illustrated by Andrew Laws,
Ramsay Gibb and Paul Sawyers
Art Editor: Rowena Alsey

Contents

MITCHELL
·BEAZLEY·

What is in Space?

When you look at the sky on a clear night, you can see the Moon and hundreds, or even thousands, of stars. The stars are part of our galaxy, called the Milky Way.

With modern telescopes and space probes, scientists are learning more about the stars and planets. They are finding out what is in space and solving some of its mysteries.

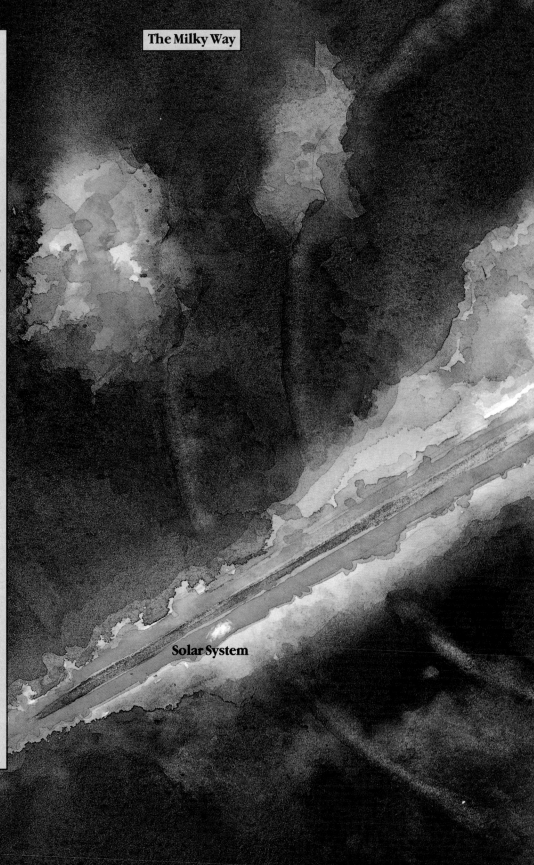

The Milky Way

Solar System

Are We Alone?

The twinkling stars you see at night are very, very far off balls of burning gases, just like our own Sun. As yet, scientists have found no other planets around stars. The Earth may be the only place in the Universe where there is life.

Clumps of Stars

The stars are in large clumps called galaxies. Our galaxy, the Milky Way, is just one of millions of galaxies in the Universe. It contains at least 100,000 million stars.

The Gigantic Universe

The Universe is very, very big. It is difficult to understand how big it really is. Even the nearest star is 400 billion km (250 billion miles) away.

Because the Universe is so big, astronomers have a special way of measuring it. They use light because it travels faster than anything else – 300,000 km (186,000 miles) a second. This is fast enough to go around the world seven times in a second.

Astronomers measure distance in light years. This is the distance light travels in one year – 9.5 billion km (nearly 6 billion miles).

The nearest star is 4.3 light years away. This means that its light took 4.3 years to reach us.

Did You Know?

Our galaxy, the Milky Way, is the shape of a giant flat bun, about 100,000 light years across. If you drove a fast car from one side to the other, it would take about 665,000 million years.

The Big Bang

Astronomers are scientists who study the Universe. They think it began about 15,000 million years ago. There was a huge explosion, called the Big Bang, which sent all the material in the Universe rushing outwards. Everything in the Universe was created out of this material, which is still moving.

No one knows what caused this huge explosion or where all the gases and dust in the Universe came from in the first place.

Astronomers hope to find out if the Universe will go on getting bigger for ever. They think it may stop one day and fall in on itself. But this will not happen for many billions of years.

The Earth and its Neighbours

The Earth is one of the nine planets which circle the Sun in our small part of our galaxy, the Milky Way. All the planets are made up of rock, metals and gases. Some have their own satellites or moons, like our Moon.

The Sun

The Sun is a star which we see during the day. Without its heat and light, there would be no life on Earth. It is a very hot ball of gas, called hydrogen, which burns with nuclear reactions at its centre.

The Sun uses up about 4 million tonnes of gas every second but it is so huge that it will shine for another 5,000 million years.

The Sun is the only object in the Solar System which gives off light. We see the Moon and the other planets because of the light from the Sun.

The Solar System

These are the nine planets in the Solar System. This shows their sizes compared to the Earth and their order from the Sun. Mercury is nearest the Sun.

All the planets are many millions of kilometres apart.

Mercury Venus Earth Mars   **Jupiter**   **Saturn**   **Uranus**   **Neptune**   **Pluto**

The Planets

Mercury is the nearest planet to the Sun. It is slightly bigger than our Moon and has almost no atmosphere to trap the Sun's heat. During the day, it is burning hot and at night it is freezing cold.

Venus lies between the Earth and the Sun. It can easily be seen without a telescope. Sometimes it looks so bright, people have thought it was a UFO.

Mars is called the Red Planet because its dry, dusty and rocky surface is red. It has huge canyons and extinct volcanoes. Its tallest volcano, Olympus Mons, is nearly three times higher than Mount Everest.

Mercury

Venus

Mars

Pluto

Pluto is an icy planet with a moon nearly as big as itself. Its orbit takes it beyond the other planets. If a jet could fly from the Earth to Pluto, it would take 1,000 years to get there.

Saturn

Uranus

Neptune

Jupiter

Rocks and Ice

As well as the nine planets circling the Sun, there are also chunks of rock, called asteroids, and lumps of rock and ice, called comets. The comets have their own orbits. Some are not seen from the Earth for hundreds of years but others return at fixed times.

Some asteroids stray into orbits nearer the Sun. If they fall through the Earth's atmosphere, most of them burn up and we see them as shooting stars. When lumps of rock or metal hit the ground, they are called meteorites.

Gas Giants

Between Mars and Pluto are the four great planets, Jupiter, Saturn, Uranus and Neptune. They are called the "gas giants", and are huge balls of gas with a rocky centre.

5

Looking into Space

Until telescopes were invented, nearly 400 years ago, no one knew very much about the Moon, stars and planets. People watched them move across the sky in the same way each year. They gave groups of stars names and told stories about them.

With telescopes, astronomers could see, for the first time, the distant stars in our galaxy, and that there are other galaxies beyond it. With huge modern telescopes they can look at stars millions of light years away and detect invisible radio waves.

Rainbow Colours

Astronomers can learn a lot about the Sun and the stars by splitting up the light from them into its different colours, like a rainbow. With a spectroscope, they can tell from the colours what gases a star is made of, how hot and far away it is and how fast it is moving.

Seeing the Invisible

Some stars give off radio waves and other waves which cannot be seen with ordinary telescopes. Radio telescopes pick up these waves with giant dishes and turn them into signals which are fed into computers.

Up in the Mountains

Many telescopes are built high up on mountains, above some of the clouds. Astronomers can see the night sky more clearly when they are far from the glare of city lights.

Mauna Kea Observatory in Hawaii, is 4,200 m (13,780 ft) up in the mountains. It is above the clouds and damp sea air.

All Done with Lenses

The first telescopes were made with two lenses, just like the lenses in spectacles. The front lens collects light from a star and focuses it on to the eyepiece lens. This magnifies the star so that it looks much larger and an astronomer can see it more clearly.

Telescopes with lenses are called refractor telescopes. The largest one in the world is at the Yerkes Observatory in the United States. It has a lens 102 cm (40 ins) across.

Taking Pictures

Many large modern telescopes can only take photographs and cannot be looked through. As each picture may take up to an hour, the telescope turns to follow a moving star. Astronomers studying the photographs have found many objects that are so faint or far away, they cannot be seen by ordinary telescopes.

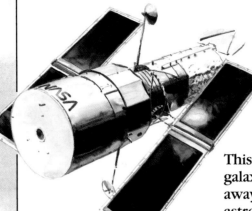

Out in Space

In 1990, America launched the Hubble Space Telescope into space. As it is outside the Earth's atmosphere, it can "see" much further into the Universe than a telescope on Earth.

This telescope can look at objects and galaxies up to 14,000 million light years away. As the light took that time to reach us, astronomers will learn what the Universe looked like 14,000 million years ago.

At Cambridge, in Britain, radio telescopes are linked together so they work like one huge telescope. Mounted on tracks, they can be moved to pin-point distant objects.

Did You Know?

The largest radio telescope is Arecibo, in Puerto Rico. Built in a bowl in the mountains, it is 300 m (984 ft) across. It can pick up radio energy which is so weak that it would take several years to collect as much as a flea uses to make a single hop.

The world's lowest telescope is 1,550 m (1 mile) down a mine in South Dakota, USA. A huge tank of cleaning fluid traps atomic particles from the Sun so they can be counted by astronomers.

The largest reflecting telescope is in the Caucasus Mountains, USSR. Its biggest mirror is so heavy, it bends under its weight of 70 tonnes. With it, you could see a candle flame 24,000 km (15,000 miles) away.

All Done with Mirrors

Huge modern telescopes have mirrors to collect light from distant stars. An astronomer looks through an eyepiece on the side of the telescope. These are called reflecting telescopes.

At the Mount Palomar Observatory in California, USA, is a giant reflecting telescope. Its mirror is 508 cm (200 ins) across, set at the end of a 110 tonne tube.

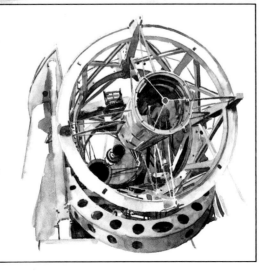

Blasting into Space

Getting into Space is not easy. The Earth's gravity, which pulls everything towards it and keeps everything on Earth in place, is very strong. Anything that goes up into the air, always comes down again.

Only rockets have powerful enough engines to blast off the ground and away from the Earth. With special fuel, they can reach the enormous speeds needed to escape from the Earth's gravity and into Space.

The First Rockets

The first rockets were worked by gunpowder and were set off by Chinese soldiers about 700 years ago. They were also used by other armies in Europe about 200 years ago.

About 90 years ago, a Russian school teacher, called Konstantin Tsiolkovskii, worked out how to make a rocket travel fast enough to get into Space. He suggested using two liquified gases, hydrogen and oxygen, as the only fuels powerful enough to drive a rocket.

The first liquid-fuelled rocket was built by an American, Robert H. Goddard, in 1926. It was 3.6 m (12 ft) long and reached a height of just over 12 m (40 ft). Later, larger rockets were built and some were used during World War II.

In 1957 the USSR launched a rocket into Space and put the first artificial satellite into orbit around the Earth. This was the beginning of the Space Race between the USA and the USSR to land on the Moon and to have manned space stations.

The Giant Saturn V

The biggest rocket ever built was the American Saturn V. Standing 111 m (364 ft) high, it carried the Apollo 11 command and service modules for the first landing on the Moon.

Saturn V was a three-stage rocket, each stage having its own engines and fuel. In all, the rocket's flight lasted only 12 minutes before sending the 43 tonne space ship on its way to the Moon.

Ariane

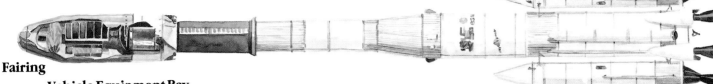

Fairing

Vehicle Equipment Bay

Third Stage   **Second Stage**   **First Stage**   **Strap-on Boosters**

The first European Ariane rocket took off in 1979. By 1990 another 35 rockets had been launched. They carry satellites and put them into orbit around the Earth. Up to three large satellites or 12 small ones can be taken up at a time.

Ariane 4 is 58 m (190 ft) long and weighs 470 tonnes. Two or four booster engines are strapped on to the main engine. They give extra lift for heavy loads at the start of a flight. When the rockets have used their fuel, they are released and fall away.

Huge Engines

The first stage of Saturn V had five giant engines, each with its own nozzle.

Lift-off began when the engines were started. Gases from over 450 tonnes of burning fuel were forced out of the giant nozzles, raising the speed of the rocket to 9,000 kph (5,600 mph). Only 2½ minutes after lift-off, it fell away 61 km (38 miles) up over the Atlantic.

Did You Know?

To escape from the pull of Earth's gravity, a rocket has to reach a speed of 11.2 km (7 miles) a second. If it was launched at this speed, it would burn up in the Earth's atmosphere.

When the Ariane takes off, it reaches a height of 100 km (61 miles) above the Earth after only four minutes.

The first living thing to be sent into Space was a Russian dog called Laika. She orbited the Earth for a week until the oxygen in the satellite was used up.

Rocket engines have their own supply of oxygen gas. There is no oxygen in Space and nothing can burn without it.

When a fully-loaded Saturn V rocket was launched from the Kennedy Space Centre in 1967, its roar shook nearby buildings. The roof of a television centre 5 km (3 miles) away fell in.

9

Training an Astronaut

Nearly 400 people had flown in space by the end of 1990. About 12 of them were women. The first space fliers were all highly-trained military test pilots. Today's astronauts have different work to do in space and many are engineers, scientists and doctors of medicine.

Anyone who has flown in space becomes a member of the most exclusive club in the world, the Association of Space Explorers. They meet each year at different places around the world.

Training for Space

It is very difficult to train astronauts to become used to the weightlessness of Space. This is because there is nowhere on Earth that is not affected by gravity.

Americans and Russians fly in a special aircraft which dives at speed, giving them up to a minute of weightlessness. The Americans call theirs "The Vomit Comet".

"The Right Stuff"

The first American astronauts were test pilots. To be selected for training, they had to be: under 40 years old, less than 1.8 m (5 ft 9 ins) tall, with no major illness, and physically fit.

They also had to have a university degree, be a graduate of a test pilot school, have 1,500 hours of flying time, be a qualified test pilot and a citizen of the USA.

The first seven chosen for the Mercury project, the first manned space flights, were supermen with special qualities, called "the right stuff."

Space Problems

About half of all the people who have flown in Space have space sickness. This is like car or sea sickness but they usually feel better after a few days.

The weightlessn1ess in Space affects the circulation of an astronaut's blood. It tends to collect around a person's middle and an extra amount goes to their heads, making their faces look puffy.

10

Dressed for Space

Astronauts wear ordinary clothes when they are in a space craft or on a space station. They put on space suits to work outside them or when landing on the Moon.

Radio Antenna

Helmet

Portable
Life Support
System

Visor

Chest Control Panel

Gloves

Space Boots

Space Suits

The bulky suit is made of many layers of special material, with a network of tubes. It protects an astronaut from radiation, keeps him warm in freezing Space and stops him getting too hot. It keeps the right pressure on his body and supplies him with air.

A space helmet has a visor to protect an astronaut from the rays of the Sun. It is fitted with a microphone and headphones so that he can talk to other astronauts or to space craft.

The backpack, called the Portable Life Support System, holds oxygen for breathing and water for cooling. On the front of the space suit is a control panel with lights to warn an astronaut when he is running out of oxygen or water.

Getting About

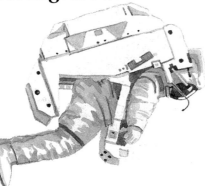

Astronauts working outside the Space Shuttle use a Manned Manoeuvring Unit, called "the armchair", to move about in Space. Small jets of gas controlled by the astronaut, push it along in the direction he wants to go.

Did You Know?

The first man to travel in space was Yuri Gagarin on 12 April, 1961. His Russian spacecraft, Vostok 1, made one orbit of the Earth in 98 minutes.

Astronauts grow a little taller in Space. Without the pull of gravity, the bones in their backs move apart. They shrink again when back on the Earth.

Mysteries of the Moon

The Moon is the Earth's nearest neighbour in Space. You can often see it clearly at night. Starting as a full moon, it changes a little each night until it disappears altogether. A few days later, a small crescent appears again.

From Earth we see only one side of the Moon. As it orbits the Earth, the Moon keeps the same side facing the Earth. No one had ever seen the other side until the Russian space rocket Luna 3 flew around it and photographed it in 1959.

Looking at the Moon

Astronomers knew that the Moon was dry and rocky. But they did not know, until the first rocket crash-landed in 1959, it was covered with a thin layer of dust. Until then they thought that any spacecraft might disappear in dust many metres thick.

The Moon's surface is covered with many large craters. The biggest we can see from Earth is 300 km (186 miles) across and has cliffs around it which are up to 4,250 m (14,000 ft) high.

Moon Prints

As there is no weather on the Moon and the Sun always shines, the Moon's surface does not get worn away. Footprints in the dust made by American astronauts will be there in millions of years' time.

On the Moon

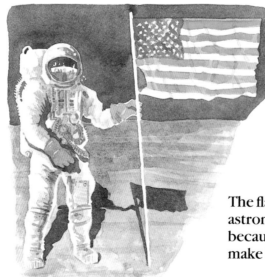

Astronauts have to wear space suits when they are on the Moon. The suits keep them cool, supply them with air to breathe, and are pressurized. As there is no air pressure, astronauts would die without them.

The flag, put up by American astronauts, is held out by a bar because there is no wind to make it fly.

Moon Facts

The Moon is 384,000 km (239,000 miles) away. A fast car, travelling non-stop from the Earth, would take 100 days to reach it.

The Moon is kept in its orbit around the Earth by the pull of the Earth's gravity. The Moon's gravity has an effect on the Earth, pulling the seas in and out, making the tides.

You can see dark patches on the Moon. In the past, people thought they were water and called them "seas". But the Moon is dry, it never rains and nothing can grow there.

The Moon has no light of its own. The light we see is reflected from the Sun. The Moon seems to change each night because we see the part that is in sunlight while the rest is in shadow.

Two American astronauts made the first Moon landing in 1969 from Apollo 11. Watched on television by people all over the world, they spent just over two hours there before returning safely to Earth.

There have been six Moon landings, all by American astronauts. On the last trips, they explored the Moon in their battery-operated Lunar Rover, taking photographs and collecting rocks and soil.

Did You Know?

If an athlete on the Moon could jump without a space suit, he could make a leap over 10 m (33 ft) high. This is because there is very little gravity on the Moon.

People living thousands of years ago were very puzzled that the Moon changed shape each night. They believed it rode across the sky in a boat and was slowly swallowed by a giant snake.

Flying the Shuttle

The rockets fired into Space can only be used once and cost millions of dollars. The American Space Shuttle can be used again and again, taking off like a rocket and landing like a glider.

It is flown by astronauts who orbit around the Earth, launching satellites and making all sorts of experiments. Each mission lasts about seven days and usually has a crew of eight.

The Stack

When a Shuttle is ready on the launchpad, it is called The Stack. The outside tank holds two supercold gases, oxygen and hydrogen. They are so cold, they are liquids. When they are brought into contact, they burst into flames.

Each Shuttle has three main engines. Their power can be revved up, like a car engine, and they can be moved to change the direction of the Shuttle.

During lift-off, 14,100 gallons of oxygen and 37,000 gallons of hydrogen are pumped from the tank into the main engines each minute.

Cockpit

Orbiter

Solid Rocket Boosters

Main Engines

The Orbiter

About as long as a big airliner, most of the Orbiter is taken up by the gigantic cargo bay. It can carry two satellites, weighing 30 tonnes — that is about as much as 60 elephants.

The large delta-shaped wings on the Orbiter help it to glide back to Earth and to manoeuvre when it comes in to land. By that time, all its rocket fuel has been used up.

Lift-off

Each Space Shuttle has three main parts. The Orbiter is about the size of a large airliner. The large outside tank holds all the fuel for the main engines. The two Solid Rocket Boosters help to blast the Shuttle into orbit around the Earth.

Two minutes after lift-off, the two Solid Booster Rockets are empty and are dropped. They fall into the Atlantic where they are picked up by ship. They are the largest things ever to come down by parachute. At Cape Canaveral they are cleaned and used again.

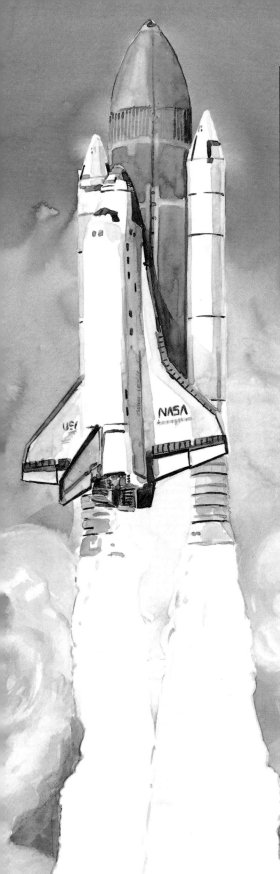

The Cockpit

The crew live and work in the Cockpit, at the front of the Orbiter. The Commander, pilot and two flight engineers sit on the flight deck for take-off.

Flight Deck

Lower Deck

The rest of the crew sit on the lower deck. Meals are heated up three times a day in the kitchen. The food is moist or compressed so crumbs do not float about.

It is warm and comfortable in the Cockpit. There is a bedroom with bunks and sleeping bags so the crew can tie themselves in. There is also a lavatory.

Did You Know?

The first Shuttle was named Constitution but so many Star Trek fans wrote in about it that NASA changed it to Enterprise.

After lift-off, the Shuttle reaches a speed of 7.5 km (4.7 miles) per second and a height above the Earth of 111 km (70 miles) in just over 8.5 minutes.

The Shuttle lands back on Earth at a speed of 344 kph (215 mph). A commercial airliner lands at about 240 kph (150 mph).

Each Shuttle Orbiter is controlled by five on-board computers during lift-off and re-entry. Four work together with one as a back-up. They must all agree but if one disagrees, the fifth one is brought in. The very first Shuttle was delayed because one computer had a time difference of 40 thousandths of a second.

When the Shuttle returns to Earth, the Commander lowers the landing wheels. If he forgets, the computers will do it for him.

Eyes and Ears in the Sky

Over 4,000 artificial satellites have been launched into Space. They orbit the Earth taking photographs, using sensors, relaying messages and sending out different signals. Carried by rockets, the satellites have been sent up by the USA, the USSR, France, Japan, China and other countries.

The Forecasters

Some satellites collect information about the world's weather and send it to computers on the ground. Satellites, called Meteosats, spin 100 times each second, scanning a small part of the Earth. They build up a picture every 25 minutes and send it to Earth every 30 minutes.

The Meteosats also collect information about the weather which is sent out by automatic weather stations, buoys floating on the sea, and by aircraft.

Weather forecasters, called meteorologists, put information from Space together with that picked up on Earth. We see the results as weather forecasts on television.

Weather forecasts tell us that it might rain tomorrow. They also warn farmers of frosts, which could damage their crops. They tell ships where there is bad weather so they can change course to avoid it and save fuel.

Ice Spotting

Satellites are used to spot icebergs and pack ice. Ships on the Great Lakes in the USA were often stranded by the ice in winter. Now satellites find clear shipping lanes through the ice and the ships are able to move along them.

16

As it Happens

Communications satellites relay telephone calls and television programmes. Stations on the ground beam radio signals to the satellites which bounce them back to other stations. With these satellites, we can watch "live" sports and news programmes.

Space Cameras

Some satellites scan the Earth with special cameras. They show up such things as rocks with useful minerals, ocean currents and areas of pollution. They are also used to improve maps and watch the growth of farm crops.

Spy in the Sky

Many countries use satellites to watch enemy ships and aircraft. They photograph military bases and rockets, and listen to radio messages. They also keep in touch with their own armed forces around the world.

Where Am I?

If you don't know where you are, you can find out from the signals from a navigation satellite. A computer on the ground can tell you to within about a metre (3 ft). These signals are used by oil rigs at sea, submarines, truck drivers in remote places and armed forces.

Did You Know?

There is a point, 35,900 km (22,309 miles) from the Earth, where a satellite seems to be fixed in the sky. This is because it is orbiting the Earth at the same rate the Earth turns on its axis.

The Earth has one natural satellite which is the Moon.

About 120,000 international telephone calls can be made at the same time, using 16 satellites and 800 ground stations.

Satellites have solar panels which collect energy from the Sun and convert it into electricity.

Remote sensing satellites orbiting the Poles 840 km (522 miles) up can spot objects on the ground the size of a large truck.

The first artificial satellite was launched in 1957 by the USSR. Called Sputnik 1, it was a metal ball, about the size of a football, and carried a radio transmitter.

Aboard a Space Station

Every 90 minutes, the first true space station goes around the Earth. It was launched in 1986 by the USSR and is called Mir, the Russian word for "peace".

Mir is one of the many Space stations where cosmonauts stay in Space for up to a year. They have to learn to live in a large room in the sky and deal with many problems.

Floating About

In a space station, there is no gravity to keep people and things in place. Cosmonauts float about, pulling and pushing themselves along by using handles. There are no chairs because there is no need to sit down.

Everything else floats about too. The cosmonauts eat food straight from packets and tubes, and drink hot or cold liquids through straws. A drink would float out of a cup and hang as a blob in the air.

To stop cosmonauts from getting bored and lonely, they have two-way television talks with friends, families and famous people. They also watch television sports and news programmes. When Mir passes over the USA, they listen to rock music on the FM radio stations.

Docking in Space

Mir is a large version of the earlier Russian Salyut space stations. Up to six detachable modules can be added on to it which act as laboratories for experiments and as a workshop. Mir will then weigh 130 tonnes.

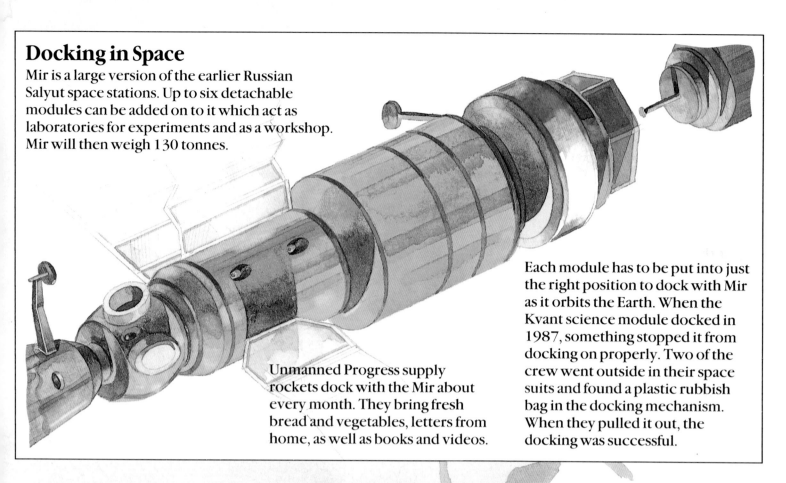

Unmanned Progress supply rockets dock with the Mir about every month. They bring fresh bread and vegetables, letters from home, as well as books and videos.

Each module has to be put into just the right position to dock with Mir as it orbits the Earth. When the Kvant science module docked in 1987, something stopped it from docking on properly. Two of the crew went outside in their space suits and found a plastic rubbish bag in the docking mechanism. When they pulled it out, the docking was successful.

Keeping Fit

In the weightlessness of a space station, people do not have to use their muscles much to move. After a few months, this affects their hearts, muscles and bones. To keep fit, cosmonauts exercise for up to three hours a day.

In the mini gym on Mir, they run on treadmills, held down by elastic ropes, and pedal exercise bicycles. Soviet doctors have invented a "suit" of stiff material which makes the wearer work very hard to stand upright.

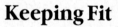

Did You Know?

On an early Salyut space station flight, the air conditioning began to go wrong. A cosmonaut radioed mission control and said, "Can we come home now? There's green mould halfway up the wall."

Two cosmonauts were supposed to report on how an onion was growing in a space station. When they did not answer questions, ground control realized they had eaten it.

The Russians are welcoming anyone to visit Mir. For about $15 million they will train two crew members and put one of them aboard Mir for eight days.

Cosmonauts may, one day, spend up to 18 months on Mir. This would be long enough for a mission to Mars and back.

Voyage to the Giants

The greatest scientific adventure, some scientists believe, began in 1977 when two Voyager spacecraft were launched. They were on a two-year journey to Jupiter and Saturn.

Later, the Voyagers also passed Uranus and Neptune. They sent back masses of data and thousands of television pictures about these very distant giant planets.

Looking Back

In 1990, Voyager 1 took 65 photographs looking back towards the Sun. These have been put together to make one picture of all the planets, except Mercury, Mars and Pluto. This wonderful picture of the Solar System is 30 m (98 ft) high and 45 m (148 ft) long.

The Voyagers

When Voyager 1 and 2 were launched, the four planets they were to visit were lined up in a special way. This will not happen again for 135 years.

Each Voyager weighs nearly 2 tonnes and is controlled by an on-board computer which is fed new programs from Earth.

Both spacecraft have worked well, although Voyager 2 suffered from wear and tear. It was slightly "deaf" when it reached Neptune after nearly 3 billion km (1.8 billion miles) 12 years later. But it was still only four minutes late.

The Voyagers have a "dish" 12 m (39 ft) across to receive signals from Earth and send back scientific results. Its signals have a power of between 6 and 23 watts – much less than an ordinary light bulb.

Voyager Facts

Both Voyagers will wander on through our galaxy for thousands of years. In 40,000 years' time, Voyager 1 will reach a dwarf star called AC +79 3888. Voyager 2 will pass close to the star Sirius in 360,000 years' time.

In case any aliens find the Voyagers, they carry a well-packed video disc and a machine to play it on. The disc contains 115 pictures of life on Earth, and recordings of sounds, music and 60 different languages.

Both Voyagers are now speeding out of the Solar System at a speed of 19 km (12 miles) a second. At this speed they would go around the world in one hour.

Jupiter

Two years after their launch, the Voyagers passed Jupiter and Saturn. Jupiter is the largest planet in the Solar System and its centre is hotter than the surface of the Sun.

It has 16 moons, four of them about the size of our Moon and larger. Two, called Ganymede and Callisto, are covered with craters. Europa has a yellow, icy crust and Io has at least eight volcanoes.

Uranus

When Voyager 2 flew past Uranus in January 1986, the planet looked blue because it was hidden in a very thick blanket of "smog".

Uranus has five icy moons. The smallest, Miranda, is covered with icy cracks and canyons, and has cliffs nearly 20 km (12 miles) high.

Saturn

You can see the rings around Saturn with a telescope. The Voyagers showed that these giant rings are really millions of ringlets and seem to be made of ice and rock.

Neptune

Voyager 2 found that Neptune has three lumpy rings. Its largest moon, Triton, is icy with a pink frost around its south pole. There seem to be lakes of a frozen gas, methane, and some icy volcanoes. It also has a very thin atmosphere of nitrogen gas.

Did You Know?

There is an electrical current between Jupiter and its moon, Io, which has more energy than all the electrical power in the United States in any second.

Jupiter, the largest of the planets, is so big that 1,030 Earths could fit into it.

Making Use of Space

In the future, more and more people will live and work on huge space stations which orbit the Earth. They will use the weightlessness of Space for scientific and medical research, and for making new and valuable materials.

Many special satellites will be launched to look at the Earth, its pollution, crops and natural resources. Space may also be used to help solve the world's pollution problems and its need for more electricity and energy.

Space Factories

In the weightlessness of Space, cosmonauts have already made special microchips which are worth many times their weight in gold. This is because crystals can be produced without the stresses and faults caused by gravity.

In weightless Space, different metals will mix together without the faults sometimes caused by gravity. Scientists will be able to make special and useful mixes, or alloys, of metals.

Some medicines can be made much stronger and much faster in a space station than on Earth.

Jumping-off Platforms

Early in the 21st century, very large space ships will be built in weightless Space. These will be used as jumping-off platforms to carry modules to the Moon to set up a base.

When a space ship is away from the pull of Earth's gravity, it does not need much energy to head for the planets. Rockets built in Space will be sent to Mars and its two moons.

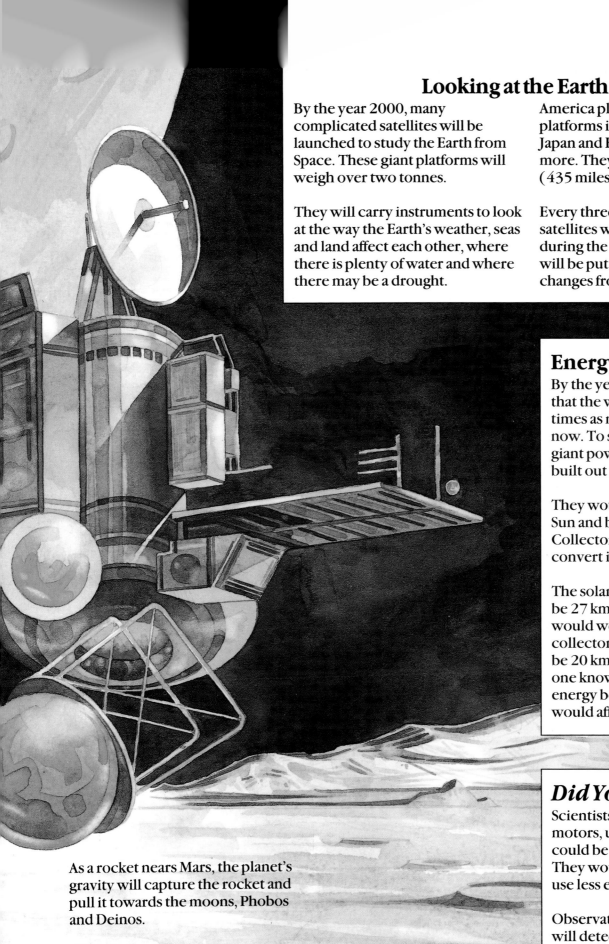

Looking at the Earth

By the year 2000, many complicated satellites will be launched to study the Earth from Space. These giant platforms will weigh over two tonnes.

They will carry instruments to look at the way the Earth's weather, seas and land affect each other, where there is plenty of water and where there may be a drought.

America plans to have six platforms in place by 2015, and Japan and Europe at least three more. They will orbit 700 km (435 miles) above the Earth.

Every three to five days, different satellites will cross the same part during the day. The information will be put together to study the changes from morning to evening.

Energy from Space

By the year 2030, it is thought that the world will need five times as much energy as it uses now. To solve this problem, giant power stations could be built out in Space.

They would trap energy from the Sun and beam it down to Earth. Collectors on the ground would convert it into electricity.

The solar power stations would be 27 km (16.8 miles) across and would weigh 60,000 tonnes. The collectors on the ground would be 20 km (12.5 miles) across. No one knows how such powerful energy beamed from Space would affect the Earth.

Did You Know?

Scientists think that electric motors, using special metals, could be made in space factories. They would be small, light and use less electricity.

Observation platforms in space will detect icebergs and ice packs on the Earth's seas. Ships will change course to avoid them and to save money.

As a rocket nears Mars, the planet's gravity will capture the rocket and pull it towards the moons, Phobos and Deinos.

Space Station Freedom

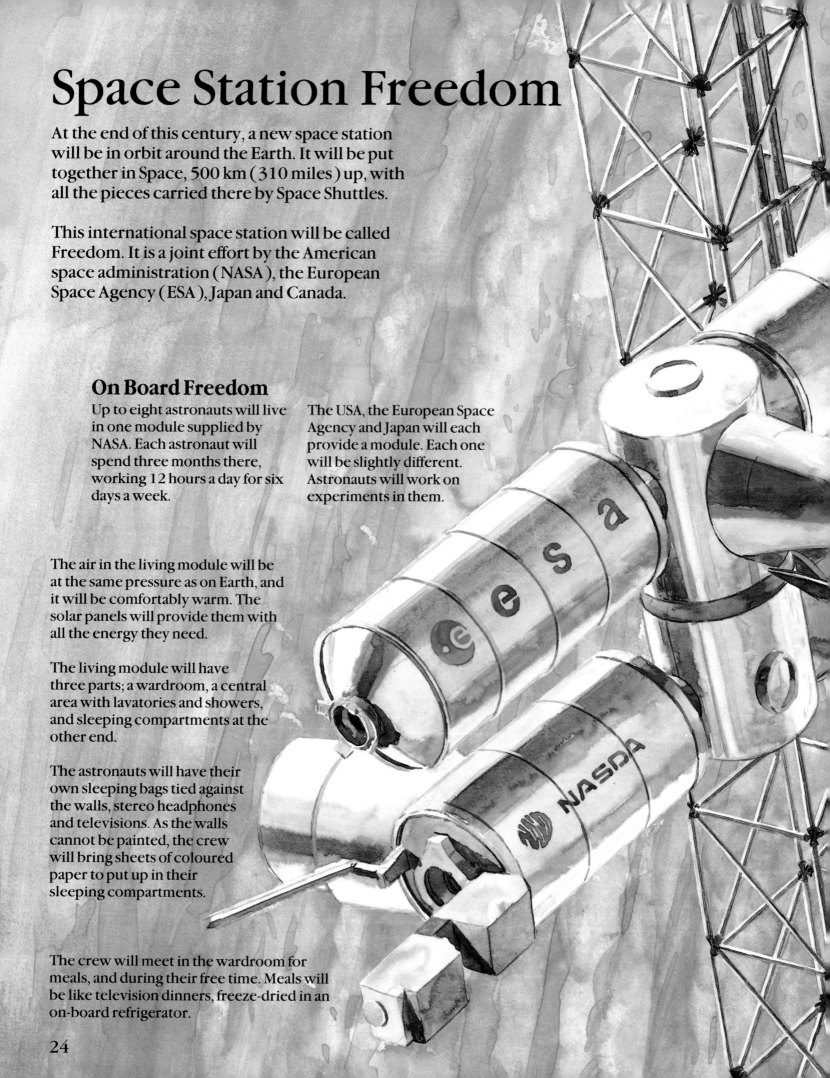

At the end of this century, a new space station will be in orbit around the Earth. It will be put together in Space, 500 km (310 miles) up, with all the pieces carried there by Space Shuttles.

This international space station will be called Freedom. It is a joint effort by the American space administration (NASA), the European Space Agency (ESA), Japan and Canada.

On Board Freedom

Up to eight astronauts will live in one module supplied by NASA. Each astronaut will spend three months there, working 12 hours a day for six days a week.

The USA, the European Space Agency and Japan will each provide a module. Each one will be slightly different. Astronauts will work on experiments in them.

The air in the living module will be at the same pressure as on Earth, and it will be comfortably warm. The solar panels will provide them with all the energy they need.

The living module will have three parts; a wardroom, a central area with lavatories and showers, and sleeping compartments at the other end.

The astronauts will have their own sleeping bags tied against the walls, stereo headphones and televisions. As the walls cannot be painted, the crew will bring sheets of coloured paper to put up in their sleeping compartments.

The crew will meet in the wardroom for meals, and during their free time. Meals will be like television dinners, freeze-dried in an on-board refrigerator.

Robot Arms

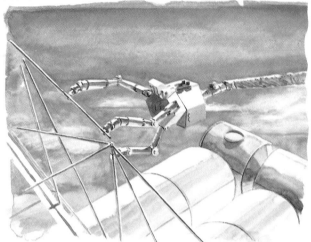

New, specially designed robot arms will be used to put together new framework on the outside of the space station. They will be controlled by the astronauts working inside the space station.

On the Japanese experiment module, there will be a robot arm to help unload materials delivered by the Shuttles. As the robots are developed, they will be able to carry out more difficult work.

Mini-Shuttles

The European Space Agency and Japan will launch space vehicles which are like small Space Shuttles. Called Hermes and Hope, they will be used to carry equipment to Freedom and for experiments.

Hermes will be launched from French Guiana and will carry three crew members. About 18 m (60 ft) long, with a wingspan of 10 m (33 ft), it will use boosters to blast it into Space.

Hope will be launched from northern Japan and will carry materials and experiments to and from the Japanese experiment module on the Freedom space station.

Did You Know?

Supplies of water and oxygen will be recycled on the Freedom space station. Without recycling, a Space Shuttle would have to deliver a full load of water every three months. Astronauts will wash their clothes in washing machines with driers. They will only be able to take one set of clothes with them to save space on board the Shuttles.

When Freedom was first planned in 1984, the price was $8 billion. NASA thinks it will cost twice as much but many scientists think it will be even more.

Into the Future

When scientists talk about what might happen in Space in the future, many people think they are cranks. The first liquid-fuelled rocket was launched by an American, Robert H. Goddard, in 1926. He said that a rocket could be sent quite easily to the Moon but many people thought this was nonsense. What seems to be impossible now, may come true one day.

Hopping Around the World

A satellite weighing one tonne needs five tonnes of fuel to launch it into orbit around the Earth. When the fuel tanks are empty, they are useless weight.

In the 1980s, Alan Bond, a British space engineer, designed a vehicle that used oxygen in the atmosphere as part of the fuel. It is called the Hotol — Horizontal Take-Off and Landing.

France, Germany, the United States, the Soviet Union, Japan and India are now racing to build "air-breathing" hypersonic planes. They would take off from ordinary runways and rush upwards into orbits reaching speeds of up to 25 times that of sound. No aircraft has ever flown so fast.

Mining in Space

Between the orbits of Mars and Jupiter is a belt of asteroids. There may be over 3,000 pieces of asteroid which did not quite form into a planet.

Scientists think that some of the asteroids may contain metals, such as iron, nickel, cobalt, titanium and aluminium. These could be mined by robots and brought back to Earth by unmanned rockets.

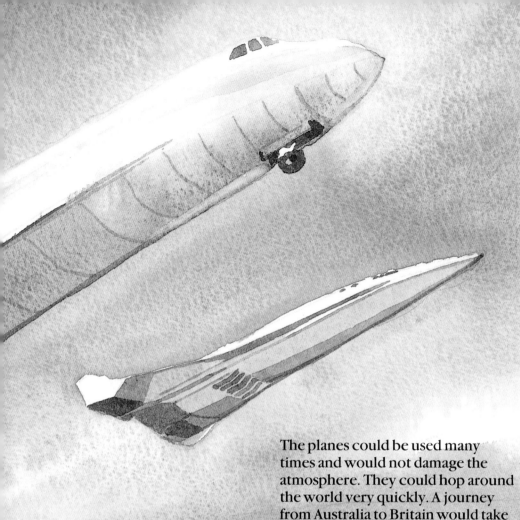

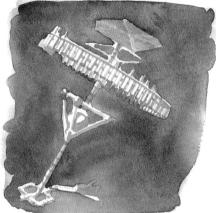

Holidays in Space

A Japanese company has designed a hotel in Space where 64 people could stay for six days at a time. The hotel looks like a giant ferris wheel on its side, which spins very quickly to create artificial gravity.

The guests would go for space walks, play games and take photographs of the Earth. Each room would have a sofa bed, a special lavatory and shower, windows with blinds and a large television monitor.

The first hotel in orbit around the Earth would be built with materials mined on the Moon. A return ticket to the hotel would cost about $45,000.

New materials will be needed for these planes and new engines, called scramjets, will have to be built to reach these speeds.

The planes could be used many times and would not damage the atmosphere. They could hop around the world very quickly. A journey from Australia to Britain would take one hour, instead of 24 hours.

Sailing with Sunlight

There have been several ideas on how to reach the asteroids. One is that solar sails would use the pressure of sunlight to move about.

A British company has suggested a sail that would unfurl like a piece of folded paper. The sail would be 60 km (37.5 miles) across and would travel at 60 kph (37.5 mph). A robot with mining tools would be dropped on to an asteroid to start mining it.

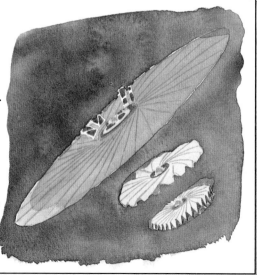

Did You Know?

There have been many ideas for holidays in space. In 1969, an airline booked seats on the first commercial flight to the Moon, although no one knew when this would be.

If an asteroid hit the Earth, it would cause terrible damage. An object only 500 m (1,640 ft) across would make a very deep crater nearly 20 km (12 miles) across.

Mysteries of Space

With wonderful new instruments and the latest techniques, astronomers are learning more and more about the Universe. But there are still many mysteries to solve about the stars and if there is any other life in the Universe.

New Stars

A star is born, after thousands of years, when enough dust and gas has collected together for the core to heat up. It cannot happen without dust, although there is only a tiny amount of dust between the stars in our galaxy. A star is ringed by dust and gas which may, one day, clump together to form new planets.

This seems to be happening to a star called Beta Pictoris, which is 80 light years away. Astronomers can see a disc of material in the star's cloud of dust, 80 billion km (50 billion miles) across. Planets may be forming at the disc's centre.

Using powerful telescopes placed in orbit around the Earth, astronomers may find out more about planets forming around stars.

Death of a Star

When a star has used up all its fuel, after many millions of years, it dies. There is a huge explosion and it collapses in on itself. All the material is crushed together in a small area, no more than 20 km (12$\frac{1}{2}$ miles) across. It is so heavy a piece the size of a pin head would weigh about a million tonnes.

These dead stars, called pulsars, spin around very quickly and give off bursts of radio waves. The radio waves are picked up by radio telescopes on Earth. About 300 have been discovered so far.

Quasars

The further away a galaxy is from the Earth, the more difficult it is to see. Some of the most distant objects seen by astronomers are the brightest. These are called Quasi-Stellar Objects or Quasars.

Most quasars look like blue stars near the edge of the known Universe. But they are much brighter than nearby galaxies and give off many hundreds more times the heat or infra-red radiation than a whole galaxy. Astronomers have no idea what they are or why they are so powerful.

Is Anyone Out There?

In October, 1992, the American space administration, NASA, will try to find out if there is any life anywhere in the Universe.

Scientists will use an electronic analyser to search for alien people. About the size of a refrigerator, the analyser will scan billions of radio waves every second for radio signals from an intelligent source.

The Arecibo telescope in Puerto Rico will look at stars which astronomers think have planets around them. Other radio telescopes, such as those used to track the Voyager spacecraft, will survey the whole sky.

No one knows what the answer will be but if ET phones home, NASA hopes to hear him do it!

Black Holes

Astronomers believe that there are black holes in the Universe but they cannot see them. When stars three times bigger than the Sun die, they collapse so quickly that no material, not even light, can escape.

Black holes can only be discovered by their effect on other stars. One of the brightest things in the sky, which puts out x-rays, is called Cygnus X-1. It orbits an invisible object which has a pull at least ten times the gravity of the Sun.

Astronomers think that this invisible object is a black hole. Material is rushing into it and it is giving off streams of x-rays.

Did You Know?

When the first pulsar was discovered, it was mistaken for alien intelligence. The signals from it were so regular that astronomers at Cambridge University in Britain called it LGM — Little Green Men. They later realized it was quite natural.

The first quasar was discovered in 1962 by Cambridge University. It has a faintly glowing "jet" of material at least 150,000 light years long. The infra-red light it puts out is over 1,000 times brighter than the Milky Way.

In 1901, a rich Frenchwoman offered a prize of 100,000 francs to anyone who could talk with a being from Space. A being from the planet Mars was not allowed as it was thought it was too easy.

Did You Know?

Bases on Mars

Mars is the planet next to Earth but it takes much longer to orbit the Sun. A Martian year, 687 Earth days long, is almost twice as long as an Earth year.

To reach Mars will take at least nine months, with a round trip of about three years. A round trip to the Moon takes a week. So far, no one has lived in Space for more than a year. Scientists think the hardest part of going to Mars will be the loneliness. They do not know how astronauts will cope with being shut up in what is little more than a large tin can.

Giant Sunshade

Scientists have suggested that a giant mirror, 2,000 km (1,245 miles) across, could be built in Space. It would reflect sunlight away from the Earth and lower the world temperature by about 4°C (7°F). This would help to solve the problem of rising world temperatures which are caused by pollution of the atmosphere.

Space Junk

Astronomers have known for a long time that Space is not quite empty. There are many meteoroids and pieces of comets, left over when the planets were born.

Now there is much more junk in Space. There are clouds of spent rockets stages, useless satellites, pieces of broken satellites and flecks of paint. Even tools and lens caps have been dropped by astronauts.

A video linked to a telescope in the USA has found more than 40,000 pieces of junk orbiting the Earth. When they crash into each other, they break up into even more, smaller pieces.

The only known casualty of space junk was a Cuban cow. It was killed in 1962 when a rocket veered off course from Cape Canaveral. The Cubans called the accident an example of American aggression and gave the cow a full, state burial.

Visitors from Space?

For hundreds of years, people have claimed they have seen strange-shaped space craft in the sky, lights moving at incredible speeds and aliens landing on the Earth. Most of these sightings have been explained but some are still unsolved mysteries.

In 1947, the pilot of a plane flying over the Rocky Mountains in the USA, reported that he saw gleaming discs in the sky. He said they were skipping across the water like saucers. Since then, UFOs, Unidentified Flying Objects, have been called "flying saucers".

Martian City?

The Viking 1 space probe orbited Mars in 1976. Later, an Italian writer in Milan claimed the probe had discovered a vast undergound city but that NASA did not release the news. He has not explained how he got this amazing information.

Space Research

Weightlessness in Space affects the bones of astronauts. They lose calcium and become brittle. The same thing happens to many people on Earth, especially women, when they grow old. If scientists can find out why this happens to astronauts, they will be able to help old people with bones that break easily.

Radiation from the Sun and from other places in the galaxy is very dangerous to astronauts. By studying the effects of radiation, scientists may learn more about cancer and the body's natural defence against it.

Getting Heavier

The Earth gets heavier by about 25 tonnes every day. This is because very fine dust, too small to see, lands on it from Space.

Iron from Space

People in Greenland made tools with iron from three very large meteorites which landed there thousands of years ago. In 1897, an American explorer, Robert Peary, took the biggest meteorite back to New York. It weighed 34 tonnes and is now in the Museum of Natural History.

Nuclear Fuel

A special form of the gas helium, helium 3, streams from the Sun on to the surface of the Moon. It could be used as a more efficient and cleaner fuel for nuclear power stations but it is very rare on Earth. A tonne of helium 3 is worth about $1 billion at today's prices.

Living on the Moon

Living on the Moon will not be very comfortable. There is no atmosphere and no cloud to shield it from the heat of the Sun. At night, the temperature is as low as −170°C (−338°F). During the day, it is as hot as 115°C (239°F).

A lunar "day" lasts for 28 Earth days. Anyone at a lunar base will have two weeks of baking Sun followed by two weeks of freezing nights when there is no Sun.

The Planets

These are the planets, in order from the Sun.

Mercury
4,900 km (3,000 miles) around its equator
58 million km (36 million miles) from the Sun
Spins once every 59 days
Orbits the Sun every 88 days

Venus
12,100 km (7,500 miles) around its equator
108 million km (67 million miles) from the Sun
Spins once every 243 or 244 days
Orbits the Sun every 225 days

Earth
12,756 km (7,926 miles) around at the Equator
150 million km (93 million miles) from the Sun
Spins once every 24 hours
Orbits the Sun every 365.5 days

Mars
6,800 km (4,200 miles) around its equator
228 million km (142 million miles) from the Sun
Spins once every 25 hours
Orbits the Sun every 687 days

Jupiter
143,000 km (89,000 miles) around its equator
778 million km (480 million miles) from the Sun
Spins once every ten hours
Orbits the Sun every 11.85 years

Saturn
120,000 km (75,000 miles) around its equator
1,427 million km (886 million miles) from the Sun
Spins once every $10\frac{1}{4}$ hours
Orbits the Sun every 29.45 years

Uranus
52,000 km (32,300 miles) around its equator
2,870 million km (1,783 million miles) from the Sun
Spins once every 16-28 hours
Orbits the Sun every 84 years

Neptune
48,000 km (30,000 miles) around its equator
4,500 million km (2,800 million miles) from the Sun
Spins once every 18-20 hours
Orbits the Sun every 165 years

Pluto
About 3,000 km (1,900 miles) around its equator
Averages 5,970 million km (3,700 million miles) from the Sun
Spins once every 6.4 days
Orbits the Sun every 248 years

Index

Edited and designed by Mitchell Beazley International Ltd. Artists' House, 14-15 Manette Street, London W1V 5LB.

© Mitchell Beazley Publishers 1991

British Library Cataloguing in Publication Data for this book are available from the British Library.

Although all reasonable care has been taken in the preparation of this book, neither the Publishers, contributors or editors can accept any liability for any consequence arising from the use thereof or from the information contained therein.

Typeset in Garamond ITC by Tradespools Ltd, Frome.
Reproduction by Mandarin Offset, Hong Kong.
Produced by Mandarin Offset.
Printed and bound in Hong Kong.